spot

OCEAN ANIMALS

PAWTUCKET PUBLIC LIBRARY

S0-AFH-807

510 2307

PAWTUCKET PUBLIC LIBRARY

DATE DUE

CRABS

by Mari Schuh

AMICUS | AMICUS INK

legs

shell

Look for these words and pictures as you read.

eyestalks

claw

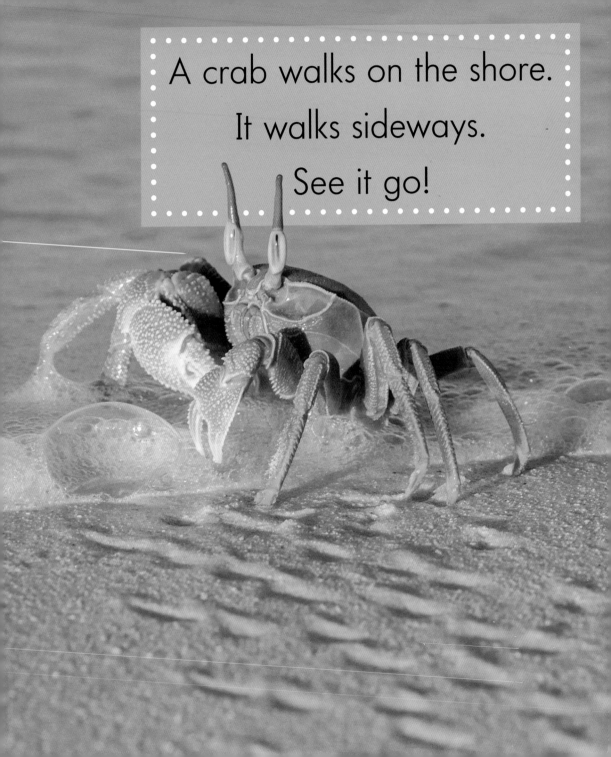

A crab walks on the shore.

It walks sideways.

See it go!

legs

Look at its legs.
They are long.
Joints help the legs bend.

3 1218 00510 2307

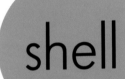

shell

Look at its shell.

It is wide and hard.

It keeps crabs safe from enemies.

eyestalks

Look at the eyestalks.
They move the eyes.
Crabs see all around.

claw

Look at the claw.

Crabs have two claws.

They grab and fight.

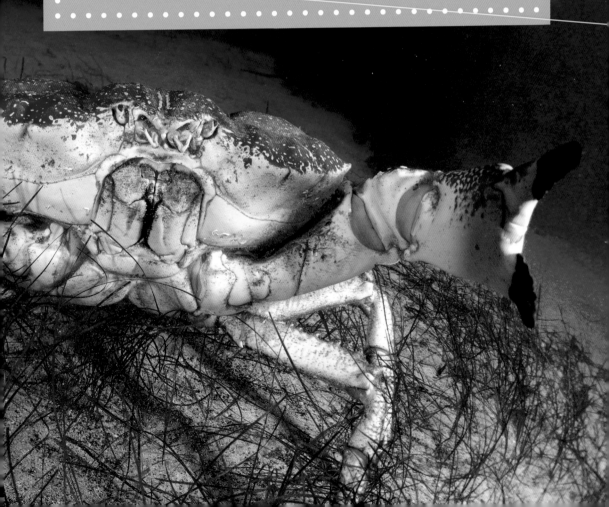

Crabs walk on the ocean floor.
They look for food.
They dig.

A crab grabs a clam.
Time to eat!

legs

Look at its legs.
They are long.
Joints help the legs bend.

shell

Look at its shell.
It is wide and hard.
It keeps crabs safe from enemies.

legs

shell

Did you find?

eyestalks

claw

eyestalks

Look at the eyestalks.
They move the eyes.
Crabs see all around.

claws

Look at the claws.
They are called pincers.
They grab and fight.

Spot is published by Amicus and Amicus Ink
P.O. Box 1329, Mankato, MN 56002
www.amicuspublishing.us

Copyright © 2019 Amicus.
International copyright reserved in all countries.
No part of this book may be reproduced in any form
without written permission from the publisher.

Library of Congress Cataloging-in-Publication Data
Names: Schuh, Mari C., 1975- author.
Title: Crabs / by Mari Schuh.
Description: Mankato, Minnesota : Spot/Amicus, [2019] |
    Series: Ocean animals | Audience: K to grade 3. |
    Includes bibliographical references and index.
Identifiers: LCCN 2017020746 (print) | LCCN 2017029472
    (ebook) | ISBN 9781681514604 (eBook) | ISBN
    9781681513782 (library binding : alk. paper) ISBN
    9781681522982 (paperback : alk. paper)
Subjects: LCSH: Crabs--Juvenile literature.
Classification: LCC QL444.M33 (ebook) |
    LCC QL444.M33 S37 2019 (print) | DDC 595.3/86--dc23
LC record available at https://lccn.loc.gov/2017020746

Printed in China

HC 10 9 8 7 6 5 4 3 2 1
PB 10 9 8 7 6 5 4 3 2 1

To Cora –MS

Rebecca Glaser, editor
Deb Miner, series designer
Ciara Beitlich, book designer
Holly Young, photo researcher

Photos by 123RF/Narongsak
Yaisumlee, cover; Dreamstime/
Picturesbyme, 14–15, iStock/EcoPic/8–9;
iStock/ANDREYGUDKOV, 10–11,
JuniperCreek, 16; Minden Pictures/
Stephen Belcher, 1; OceanWide
Images, 4–5, 12–13; SeaPics, 3;
Shutterstock/Narong Jongsirikul, 6–7

CRABS